Lost Industr

Turton Moor

Forgotten mining and pipe making industries in a remote part of Turton

SEPTEMBER 2003

PETER HARRIS

TURTON LOCAL HISTORY SOCIETY

This publication is the twenty fourth issued by the Society, associated with the aim of promoting an interest in history and particularly the local history of Turton District by discussion, research and record.

PUBLICATIONS

Our area of interest is old Urban District of Turton, including the townships of Bradshaw, Edgworth, Entwistle, Harwood, Longworth, Quarlton and Turton. Meetings are held from September to May inclusive, at 7.30 pm on the third Tuesday of the month at the Barlow Institute, Edgworth. Visitors are welcome.

CONTENTS

MAPS AND DIAGRAMS

ILLUSTRATIONS

ACKNOWLEDGEMENTS

Thanks are due for assistance in producing this work as follows:-
Jim Francis, for suggesting the topic, finding several useful documents and providing encouragement.
Helen Heyes for, pointing out important references that I had overlooked..
Alan Davis, formerly of Lancashire Mining Museum, for making available the plan of post 1893 mining activity.
Eric Mason for providing the only photograph of the working colliery.
The Public Record Office, The Coal Authority, Darwen Public Library, Bolton Archive Service, Lancashire Record Office, Bolton Evening News.
Photographs on pages 17, 22 and 60 are taken from 'Coalmining in Salford'.

iv

View from Old Lyons Farm of the Cadshaw valley and north side of Turton Moor. The site of the original Turton Moor Colliery is at the foot of the hill in the centre of the photograph. Old Lyons Farm, like others in the area, was demolished to provide a sterile water catchment area.

Chapter 1   INTRODUCTION

Anyone who walks to the west, up the rough moorland road that rises from Blackburn Road near the junction with Green Arms Road, soon realises that it has been rather better constructed than the usual farm track. Gradients are gentle, there are no sharp bends and in places the remains of some robust stone surfacing has survived as a reminder that it was once intended to carry heavier traffic.

Eventually, after a steady climb of a mile or more, the track comes to an abrupt end in the upper Cadshaw valley amid some small circular depressions and a few irregular heaps, mostly covered in vegetation. These are the remains of the original Turton Moor Colliery that the track was constructed to serve. The circular depressions are old shafts that have been filled and the heaps are colliery spoil that has become grassed over. Once, there would, no doubt, have been at least one pithead gear, some mine buildings and stages for loading coal carts, but these have long vanished and only the earthworks remain.

Half a mile to the south, on the other side of Turton Moor, lie the remains of another Turton Moor Colliery that worked the same coal but at a later date and greater depth. By a curious coincidence some relics of this operation are shown on the current 1:25000 OS map. These include the track of an old tramway that extends over nearly a mile from Charters Moss on Blackburn Road to a point high on the southern side of Turton Moor where there is a 'disused shaft'.

Another walk, this time up the old tramway route, soon confirms that it was a well graded, narrow gauge system with an odd piece of rail and remains of sleepers still to be found. At the upper end it leads to two old shafts, now covered with concrete caps, spoil heaps and some small artificial ponds, probably to supply water for boilers and processing plant; in short the unmistakable relics of a small mine from a century ago. At the lower end of the tramway, in a dark and gloomy plantation of fir trees alongside the main road, a determined explorer will find the remains of quite a large pipe works with fragments of glazed sewer pipes, bricks and cinders lying around a substantial concreted area. This was the works of the Turton Moor Sanitary Pipe Company (Figs 1 & 2).

Motorists on the main road, passing this rather remote spot, might be surprised to realise that it was once, briefly, a substantial industrial site, with kilns, chimneys and offices, that must have been very visible in this wild moorland setting. In its heyday, at the beginning of the 20th century, Turton Moor Colliery employed 70-80 men underground in addition to others on the surface and at the pipe works. Yet no domestic housing was ever provided to serve the area. The closest accommodation would have been at Dimple or Bull Hill, or in the few nearby farms and cottages. Most of the employees must have been very familiar with long, dark winter walks to and from work in the cold and rain.

Figure 1. Mid nineteenth century map of Turton Moor and surrounding districts. Turton Moor Collieries and associated activities are located in the highlighted area.

3

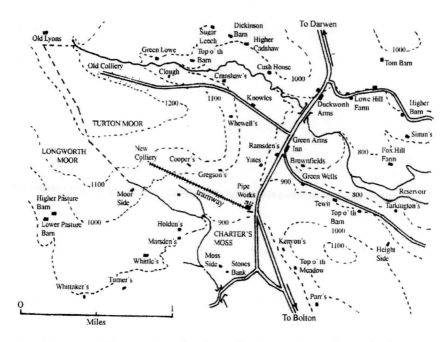

Figure 2   Map of Turton Moor showing collieries, tramway, pipeworks, farms and other major features.

Turton Moor from Entwistle Reservoir.

4

Entrance to the old colliery track from Blackburn Road nearly opposite the site of the Green Arms Inn.

The lower end of the colliery track near Blackburn Road.

The colliery track surface, still looking fairly solid, 160 years or so after construction.

The colliery track approaching the old Turton Moor Colliery. Spoil heaps close to the horizon in the centre of the photograph mark the position of the colliery.

Turton Moor from Turton Heights with Blackburn Road in front of the tree covered site of the pipe works. The line of the tramway can be seen rising to the new colliery from the pipe works.

The site of the new colliery with Winter Hill in the background. The ponds were probably for boiler water. Low stone walls surround the two shafts.

Chapter 2   COAL AT TURTON MOOR

The collieries at Turton Moor worked a seam known as the Lower Mountain Mine in the lower part of the Coal Measures where coal seams are typically less than 2 feet thick and widely separated. The Lower Coal Measures were not very attractive to work commercially and could never support operations of the size found in the main part of the coalfield, such as the area between Bolton and Salford, where a single colliery might work 6 or more seams each between 3 and 6 feet thick.

The little coalfield of Turton Moor is bounded by two major faults on its northeast and southwest sides respectively, separating it from virtually barren measures. The two faults converge to the southeast and effectively pinch out the coalfield on Charters Moss. To the north, the seam came to the surface in Cadshaw Brook close to the northeast boundary faults although it is not exposed now.

The main coal is up to 20 inches thick and associated with a thick fireclay. In the new colliery the seam inclines to the southeast at gradients of 7-8%. Further north, in the area of the old colliery, there is no unambiguous record of the seam's inclination, but the geology suggests that it inclines to the south or south west at a shallow gradient (Fig 3). Various small faults occur and these probably separate the workings of the two collieries.

The mining leases were all issued by the Lord of the Manor of Turton and only authorised extraction within that township. This might have inhibited the miners from following the seam into Longworth, although, with the lease boundary so close to the boundary fault, such an extension might not have been worthwhile.

Haulage work in an early coal mine.

8

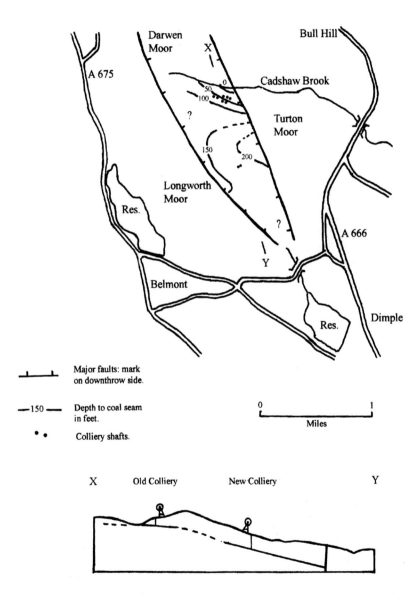

Fig 3 Map and section showing the approximate position and depth
of the Lower Mountain Mine at Turton Moor.

Chapter 3   THE FIRST TURTON MOOR COLLIERY

The existence of Turton Moor Colliery is recorded on the 6-inch Ordnance Map (Lancashire Sheet 78), surveyed between 1845 and 1847. The site, at the end of the cart road on the north side of Turton Moor, is clearly identified as 'Turton Moor Colliery' and consists of several shafts, a tunnel, a quarry and a coke kiln. Six of the shafts are described as 'old coal pits', one is a 'coal pit' and the other, near the coke oven at the furthest point reached by the mine track, is represented only by the symbol for a shaft (Fig 4). It seems that only one or two shafts would be in operation at the time of the survey while the others appeared, at least to the surveyors, to be disused or inactive.

The coke kiln would probably be of the beehive type, derelict examples of which can still be seen around Entwistle. They were primitive affairs, about 6-8 feet in diameter and of similar height, tapering towards the top and constructed of stone. The gas, and other by-products from the coking process would probably have been allowed to escape over the surrounding countryside. In the early part of the nineteenth century coke was sometimes a preferred fuel because it burned with less smoke and fume than coal. It was also used for smelting iron in blastfurnaces and for other metallurgical purposes.

The quarry would be for stone structures on the surface and roof support underground. Stone would be used because it was more readily available than wood in this area.

The tunnel, at the east end of the site, gives access from the track, near one of the large boundary faults, to some shafts on the hillside, two of which can still be distinguished (Nos. 12 & 13 Fig 6). Where the tunnel eventually goes is not entirely clear. It might incline downwards to intersect the seam under Turton Moor or it might have been a trial into measures on the east side of the fault, where various thin coal seams are recorded, although none of them were ever successfully exploited. Even the position of the fault in relation to these shafts is not known precisely, the ground nearby might well have a complex structure, and in the absence of any mine plans further speculation is not worthwhile.

The first systematic record of the colliery appears in the 'List of Mines' initially published in 1854 and then at annual intervals by the Mines Record Office of the Geological Survey. These lists show that 'Turton Moor Colliery' was worked by Andrew Knowles and Sons in 1854 and 1855 but not in 1856 or in any year thereafter until 1861, by which time the mining activity had been re-established some distance away and Andrew Knowles was no longer connected with it.

In the archive at Bolton there is a note, dated April 1849, of the industries in Turton that are assessed for poor rates. Turton Moor Colliery is listed and beside the entry is a pencil note to the effect that the mine is 13 inches deep, 10 men are employed and the quantity of coal got per week is about 90 tons. No doubt the figures for output and men employed are reliable enough, although the statement that the seam is only 13 inches thick is hard to believe, particularly as other estimates suggest 20 inches. However it is clear from the output and numbers employed that this was a small operation.

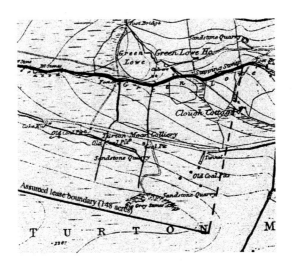

Fig 4   Workings of Andrew Knowles & Co at Turton Moor, from the 1:10560 OS map of 1847. The suggested boundary of the 148 acres mining lease is indicated.

Working in a thin seam c.1920.

A Bolton newspaper helps fill in a few more details, about what can be called the old colliery, in the form of an advertisement for a coal lease and a report of a coroner's inquest.

The 'Bolton Chronicle' of 7 August 1852 carried a notice headed 'To let: Turton Moor Colliery' which went on to describe the offer of a lease of 'all the coal under 70 Cheshire acres on Turton Moor consisting principally of a mine called Dogshaw Mine that has been worked for a number of years by Andrew Knowles and Son'. The mine is further described as being 'up good roads and within a moderate distance of the surface and may be laid dry by a fall within the estate'.

A few months later, on 26 April 1853 the same paper recorded the unfortunate deaths of Thomas Fish, underlooker and John Clegg, collier, at Turton Moor Colliery, belonging to Messrs A Knowles and Son. Apparently both of them got into the cage, to descend a shaft into the colliery, when the winding rope broke.

From these articles some useful information comes to light. For instance, Andrew Knowles had worked the same seam of coal for several years prior to 1852. He must also have succeeded in renewing the lease, advertised in 1852, otherwise he would not have been the owner the following year when the accident occurred.

It is interesting to learn that the seam was recognised as being the same as that worked at Dogshaw Colliery in Darwen. Dogshaw, now called Duckshaw, is about a mile north of Turton Moor Colliery on the east side of Darwen Moor. Although the coal cannot be followed continuously between the two places, its characteristics must have appeared sufficiently similar at both collieries for its identity to be recognised . No one since has ever doubted this correlation, only the name has changed. As the geology became better understood, it was realised that the Dogshaw Mine was the same as a seam recognised in other parts of Darwen as the Half Yard Mine and this name was eventually adopted. Later still the seam was traced to other parts of the Lancashire Coalfield where it was known as the Lower Mountain Mine, the name it now bears.

At this point, it is perhaps worth reminding those unfamiliar with the subject, that in Lancashire, coal seams are called 'mines' and coal mines 'collieries', although, perhaps perversely, the people who work in them might call themselves either colliers or coal miners.

The date when mining started at Turton Moor is not on record, but an accident is recorded in 1846 when John Holt, aged 63, was killed by a roof fall at 'Messrs Knowles colliery at Turton', which is probably Turton Moor. On the other hand, in a rating valuation of the whole of Turton township, carried out in 1837, there is no assessment for any mining activity in the area by Andrew Knowles, or indeed by anyone else, although coal mining was a rateable activity.

The Cheshire acres referred to in the lease were the traditional land measure used in mining in Lancashire until well into the nineteenth century. The difference between Cheshire and statutory land measurement lay in the perches. Cheshire perches were 8 yards long while statutory perches were only 5.5 yards long and in both cases there were 40 square perches to the rood and 4 roods to the acre. Hence one Cheshire acre was equivalent to 2.116 statutory acres and the 70 Cheshire acres mentioned in the lease are equivalent to statutory 148 acres. A seam, 20 inches thick, by traditional methods of evaluation, should contain about 2500 tons of coal per statutory acre. However by no means all the lease would contain coal and even where it did the amount of coal lost in mining and the production of unsaleable fine particles would be considerable.

The location of the 148 acre lease can be guessed at, if only because it lies in a remote corner of Turton close to the boundaries with Over Darwen and Longworth, which would act as limits. A third side of the lease is probably defined by a coal boundary, shown on a plan of the last stage of mining, which runs near the crest of Turton Moor and will be described later. The location of the remaining side of the lease can be inferred, knowing the measured area and assuming a regular outline (Fig 4). Finally it may be noted that the coal is at a 'moderate' depth and can be 'laid dry by a fall within the estate', which means that the drainage could be entirely by gravity. There was no need for a pump and presumably Andrew Knowles did not use one. A drainage tunnel from a low point in the mine to a nearby valley, within the lease area, would be sufficient to conduct the water away.

In Cadshaw Brook, below the mine, a discharge of orange coloured water is found on the south bank, which seems to mark the position of a drainage tunnel. The bank at this point has been strengthened by a substantial stone retaining wall, probably emplaced in the late 19th century, when water collection for Entwistle reservoir became important. The retaining wall has obliterated the original tunnel entrance but a small gap remains through which the orange stained stream issues, discolouring Cadshaw Brook for some 300 feet downstream. Water draining through a coal mine often dissolves iron but, when it approaches the surface and becomes aerated, the iron forms an easily recognised bright orange suspension. A discharge of this sort found in a coal mining area is a good, though not infallible, sign that water is draining from a mine.

The drain exit is at an elevation of 1075 feet and, if the 1852 advertisement about drainage is correct, this level must be slightly below the lowest point of the coal seam in the lease area, otherwise the mine would not drain naturally.

A mining plan has come to light of the workings as they were in 1850. It was probably produced to enable royalties to be assessed and shows the precise extent and superficial area of the workings. It is not a complete record of all mining at the colliery, which, of course, continued for a further 5 years after the plan was made, nor does it seem to record all working that had taken place since mining began. It also neglects to record certain desirable data like the gradient of the seam and depth of the shafts. Nevertheless it is a very valuable document and enables much to be inferred about the early workings.

Although there are no surface details on the plan, it does record the position of 5 shafts that can be correlated with the remains of 5 of the shafts currently observable alongside the mine track. These shafts, numbered 3-7 are shown superimposed on the current 1:2500 OS map together with the known underground workings (Fig 6). The other shafts mark either the progress of the working after 1850 (Nos 1,2,6 & 8) or, as they appear on the 1847 OS map, are the relics of earlier workings that were not worth recording on the 1850 plan (Nos 10 & 11).

The mine plan shows clearly that workings extended to about the crest of Turton Moor. In one place a heading has been driven even further to the south, perhaps even beyond where the lease boundary is thought to be. Where the working had finally got to by 1855, possibly under an extended lease, can only be guessed at. They obviously went further to the west beneath two of the post 1850 shafts (Nos 1 & 2) and into another area between the mine track and the river where there are two shafts of similar age (Nos 8 & 9), but how far they went to the south beyond the crest of Turton Moor is the main question. Certainly the Inspector of Mines later feared they had gone a long way in this direction when he warned of the possible presence of flooded workings, described in more detail in due course. However if the colliery did not need a pump, as was suggested in the 1852 lease advertisement, then the workings could not go below the level of the drainage tunnel, the exit of which, if it has been correctly recognised, is at 1075 feet above sea level. This factor alone could severely limit the extent of the colliery and ensure workings did not extend very far under the moor. Of course it is possible that some sort of pumping was introduced between 1852 and 1855, but there is no evidence of it and, at this early date, when rather cumbersome equipment was in use, installation would have been tedious and expensive.

Obviously the workings near the mine track were shallow. Shaft sinking is expensive, depending on the depth, and it is inconceivable that so many shafts would be provided, in such a small area, unless this was a relatively cheap and cost-effective option. It is obvious, too, that the preferred location for the shafts was alongside the track. No attempt was made to sink shafts to the south where the hillside rises steeply and the distance from the surface to the coal rapidly increases, nor were shafts located far from the track on the north side where the hillside slopes down to the river.

It is not possible to be precise about the depth of the shafts but application of the simple structural model described above suggests that they would all be mostly in the range 50-75 feet deep. The advantage in having the shafts close to the level track would lie with the easy transport of heavy loads. Andrew Knowles's main problem then would lie in reaching coal up to the limits of his lease under Turton Moor and in maintaining sufficient ventilation. At that time it was common practise to have a furnace at the bottom of an upcast shaft to drive the ventilation and it is possible that one of the shafts was so used. It is also possible that at least one of the shallower shafts was fitted with ladders as the vertical distance was quite small and ladders would allow for easy underground access.

The 1850 colliery plan indicates that a section of the seam was being worked by a Mr Garbett. The workings were in separate panels of coal arranged in such a way as to suggest that a section of the colliery had been sub-let, although Garbett's workings were still within Turton Moor Colliery, accessed through Knowles's shaft and roadways and not in any way a separate colliery.

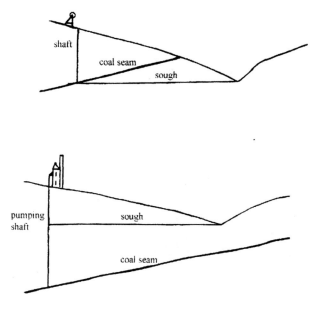

Fig 5   Diagram illustrating the use of soughs or drainage levels, either by gravity alone (upper) or with a pump (lower). The sough was constructed with the lowest possible gradient so as to drain as much coal as possible. It usually terminated close to river level in a nearby valley.

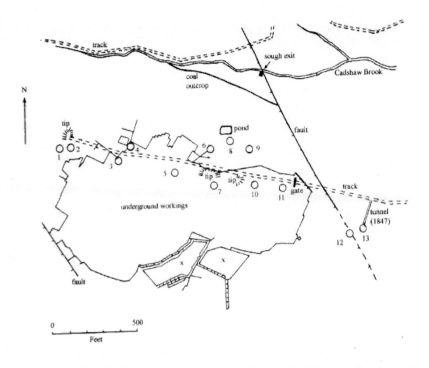

Fig 6. Turton Moor Colliery (old): the area worked until 1850 is outlined, shafts are numbered 1-13, workings by 'Mr Garbett' are indicated (x).

Title from the 1850 mine plan by Andrew Knowles.

16

Remains of Whewells Farm and view across the Cadshaw valley. The colliery track lies beyond the tree. In 1871 William Mason, a 'brickmaker' aged 19, who was probably employed at Turton Moor, lived here.

A coal cart, belonging to Andrew Knowles & Sons, turned out for a May Day procession in 1904. 50 years earlier similar carts, in less polished condition, probably provided the main traffic on the track to the old colliery.

Remains of a filled shaft at the old colliery (Shaft 12, Fig 6).

Another filled shaft at the old colliery (Shaft 6, Fig 6).

Cadshaw Brook constrained by concrete walls downstream from the colliery. The orange colour of the water is caused by iron oxides from the mine.

Orange coloured water from the colliery drain, or sough, where it joins Cadshaw Brook

The site of the old colliery from the North side of Cadshaw Brook. Shaft 7 (Fig 6) lies behind the large grass covered tip in the centre of the photograph.

The far end of the colliery track, at the site of the old colliery, on the North side of Turton Moor.

Remains of a coke oven on Cranberry Moss, Entwistle. A similar structure existed at the old colliery in the late1840s.

Old coke ovens at The Naze, Entwistle

Wheatsheaf Colliery, Pendlebury: one of the larger operations belonging to Andrew Knowles and obviously in a different league from Turton Moor.

(Upper) The early colliery (c.1863) with wooden headframes and facilities for loading coal carts directly from mine tubs.

(Lower) The same colliery in 1953, after it had become part of the National Coal Board, with totally changed surface arrangements including new steel headframes.

Chapter 4   ANDREW KNOWLES & CO.

Although the old Turton Moor Colliery was a relatively small operation, even by the standards of the times, nevertheless, as a part of the Andrew Knowles company, it belonged to a coal mining organisation of considerable size and importance.

In the 1855 list of mines, the last to include the old Turton Moor Colliery, Andrew Knowles and Son is credited with 11 separate collieries. In the Bolton area they owned the collieries known as Little Bolton, Little Lever, Quarlton, Top o' th' Lane (Darcy Lever), Hacken and Turton Moor, while nearer Manchester they owned substantial operations at Agecroft, Clifton Hall, Clifton Moss, Pendlebury and Pendleton.

The way the organisation was regarded in the mid-nineteenth century can be appreciated from an article in the trade press written only a few years after Knowles had ceased mining at Turton Moor. The occasion was the annual meeting, in Manchester, in 1861, of the British Association for the Advancement of Science, which included a visit to Andrew Knowles's operations at Pendlebury and Pendleton. The 'Colliery Guardian' took the opportunity to describe the visit at some length and to review the activities of Andrew Knowles, in the prose of the time, as follows:-

'The whole of the collieries belonging to Messrs Knowles constitute a concern greater than any in Lancashire; indeed we doubt whether there is any propriety in Great Britain that raises as large a quantity of coal; but the collieries are in different locations, so that it would be impossible to inspect even the surface arrangements of all of them in less than a week. Yet there are many of them which taken separately afford an adequate representation of the progress of coal mining in Lancashire. A better selection for a visit could not have been made, and the reception that Messrs Knowles accorded to their guests was such as to render the visit not only as useful but as pleasant as possible. Many gentlemen expressed their amazement at what they had seen at Pendleton Pit, and it was evident that some had found that coal mining in Lancashire was far more advanced than they expected and others had found the art of coal mining itself a very different thing from what they had previously supposed.

The public at large know very little of coal mining and we are afraid that the general impression is that the occupation of a collier is dirty and dangerous while the qualifications required of his employer are comprised in the possession of a very moderate amount of capital.

The scientific visitors to the collieries of Messrs Knowles must have noticed a multitude of indications of the connection between coal mining and natural philosophy. The very plans they looked at in the office at Pendlebury proved that the men who had the management of the collieries were possessed of apractical knowledge of the strata of an extensive district, and were therefore entitled to rank as experienced geologists. The arrangements for ventilation in the different mines that were visited proved their knowledge of gases and the way to deal with them and the noble steam engines, with their concomitant apparatus, which were so much admired, bore witness to the mechanical skill of those who superintended their operation.

The immense concern belonging to Messrs Knowles and Son is of real Lancashire growth; it has been built up in Lancashire fashion, by judgement, industry and frugality. The foundation was laid by the late Andrew Knowles, who started with little capital except his brains, and who left an extensive system of collieries, which under the management of his sons and grandsons has acquired such stupendous proportions that it is said they raise a larger amount of coal every year than does any other proprietary in the world.

The works of Messrs A Knowles and Sons are divided into six sections, those of Lever, Bolton, Stoneclough, Manchester, Radcliffe and Rochdale: and altogether they employ considerably over 3000 men. The gross quantity of coal raised per day is about 3000 tons, or more than a million and a half tons per annum. For raising the coal there are 90 steam engines in use, varying in size according to what they have to do. In the pits there are about 200 horses, and for the conveyance of coal to different markets there are 150 carts, 180 canal boats, and about 300 large railway wagons. The number of trams and tubs are almost beyond computation and the length of tramways above ground and underground, we shall not exaggerate in saying that it may be expressed in hundreds of miles.'

Although the 'Colliery Guardian' might occasionally have been carried away in its enthusiasm, few in the industry would have tolerated such opinions had there not been some truth in them. Andrew Knowles and Sons was one of the most advanced coal mining organisations in the world at that time. It was properly financed, well managed, had access to the latest technology and above all was highly successful over a long period. In fact, it lasted as a separate entity until the 1930s, when it merged with other coal companies in the area to become Manchester Collieries and, after further mergers, Lancashire Collieries. Eventually surviving parts of the organisation were taken into the National Coal Board.

Looking now at the site of the old colliery on Turton Moor, it is hard to see what advantage an organisation like Andrew Knowles could find in working this thin seam in such a remote location. But the firm must have known its business and the colliery would have been properly managed in the light of the economic conditions then prevailing. No doubt Andrew Knowles worked the lease as far as was profitable and probably considered acquiring further leases, but by 1855 the company seem to have had enough of Turton Moor and were content to leave further mining to other operators. Why Turton Moor Colliery, apparently profitable enough in the mid 1840s, should become unattractive in 1855, is not clear. Perhaps the opening of the Bolton to Blackburn railway, within this period, enabled cheaper supplies of coal to be delivered into the district.

After Andrew Knowles stopped working in 1855, mining equipment would have been salvaged, the shafts filled, surface structures removed and the site allowed to become derelict. There seems not to have been any closing down sale, a common enough event when a colliery reached the end of its life, perhaps the equipment was used elsewhere in the Knowles organisation.

Unloading tubs of coal from a cage at Rose Bridge Colliery, Wigan c 1900, (from Mines and Miners of South Lancashire).

Chapter 5   BRIGGS AND WALSH

After Andrew Knowles gave up mining the area lay unworked until 1861 when a Turton Moor Colliery once again appears in the official list of mines; this time under the ownership of Briggs and Walsh. The mine continued to appear in 1862 and 1863, but now apparently under the sole ownership of John Walsh. However in January 1863 the company, calling itself Walsh and Briggs, wrote to the rating assessment officer at Turton as follows:- 'We first raised coal for sale on Turton Moor on 1 March 1862, and we have sold 21 hundred tons from 1 March to 31 December at an average price of 5/4d per ton. We have eight men getting coal. You'll be as easy as you can in the assessment. You will see from the statement that we are getting a very small quantity and there are no profits but a loss.'

It seems odd that the company should achieve so little output in the first 10 months of operation. The capital outlay involved in sinking new shafts would have been considerable as would that for the winding and pumping engine and other items needed for the new colliery. There would be an urgent need to recover this money as soon as possible, an objective unlikely to be achieved from the efforts of only eight men. Either something was wrong with the mining operation, or there was little demand for the coal and production had to be restricted. Whatever the reason, the unhappy situation seems to have come to a head the following year when the whole operation including the lease, colliery and all the equipment was put up for auction in an event advertised in the 'Bolton Chronicle' of 30 January 1864.

The sale was scheduled for 18 February 1864 at the Green Arms Inn, the nearest inn to the colliery, and was conducted by Mr William Sailsbury. It included, the mine, engine, boiler, working plant and *all beds of coal under certain lands belonging to Arabella Penelope Eliza Hoare (Lord of the Manor) at or near Turton and commonly known as Turton Moor, comprising 248 acres and 27 perches or thereabouts'*. Also in the sale was *'the boiler house, smithy, pumping and hoisting fixtures, smith's working tools, fittings and gearings, ropes, chains, weighing machine, coal boxes, wagons etc. Also rails and sleepers from the pit to the cart set situated near the machine house and weighing machine adjoining the turnpike from Darwen to Bolton'*. The colliery was described as being *'a short distance from the turnpike near the Green Arms Inn, Turton'*. The mines of coal were held on a 15 year lease dating from 24 June 1858 at a yearly rent of £80 or £50 for each 7840 sq. yds of coal of one foot thickness per year or a pro rata amount for greater or lesser quantities. Further information could be had from John Walsh, farmer, Grainings, Over Darwen or Mr Ainsworth, solicitor, 32 Clayton Street, Blackburn.

26

The lease of 248 acres, held by John Walsh, was obviously larger than that originally worked by Andrew Knowles and most of it must have been to the south side of the original lease, where the coal seam extends in depth.

The existence of a tramway extending from the colliery to a weighing machine near the main road is surprising, at this early date, as it is not shown on any map and there is otherwise little sign of its existence, although a tramway was specifically included in the 1866 colliery rating valuation. The situation of the colliery, described as being a short distance from the Green Arms Inn is rather inaccurate since both the old and new colliery sites would be about a mile away from the inn. Also it is not absolutely clear, from the notice, which of the two collieries is being referred to, although the existence of pumping equipment suggests that it was the new pit, and the tramway provides confirmation. Otherwise it would be necessary to envisage almost a mile of tramway, of which there is no trace, to a colliery already served by a well engineered cart track, built by Andrew Knowles, that is still in surprisingly good condition. Official confirmation of the new shaft is provided by the first geological survey map which confirms that a new shaft, absent in 1849, was in existence before 1869.

The sinking of a 174 feet deep shaft or shafts, installation of pumps, construction of over half a mile of tramway and generally bringing a new colliery into existence seems an ambitious undertaking for a man like John Walsh, who regarded himself primarily as farmer, and so it proved. However he does deserve the credit for establishing a new colliery that lasted, in one form or another, for over forty years.

Nineteenth century advertisement for mining equipment.

The tree covered site of Green Arms Inn at the junction of Blackburn Road and Green Arms Road. The colliery lease was auctioned at the inn 1852.

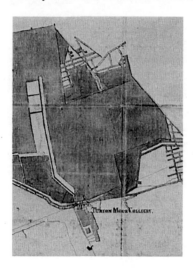

Part of the colliery plan of 1878, including buildings and tramway at the pit head.

Chapter 6   TURTON MOOR COAL (AND FIRECLAY) CO.

In 1864 Turton Moor Colliery continued to appear in the annual list of mines, although now the owners were the Turton Moor Coal Co., presumably the organisation that obtained the colliery from John Walsh. This company also appears in the press in 1865 over a court case involving payment to a subcontractor, John Entwistle of Darwen. He made a verbal contract with Mr Barns of 'Turton Colliery Co' (the reporter meant Turton Moor Colliery Co) to make a tunnel 6 feet high by 5 feet wide and 750-900 feet long at a price of 27 shillings per yard and 40 shillings per yard in rock, the work was visited by Messrs Barns, Mc Keand and Dawson (directors) and £20 paid on account, but after being driven for 138 feet it was stopped because the level in the tunnel was not correct and there was a dispute over payment.

In 1866 the *'colliery and tramway'* of the *'Turton Moor Coal and Fireclay Co.'* (the first time fireclay has been mentioned) *'in the occupation of Livesley Stock, Robert McKeand and Patrick Dawson'* were valued for rating purposes at £95. Later in that year the company again appeared in the newspaper, this time in the form of a notice of dissolution of a partnership in the *'Turton Moor Coal and Fireclay Co'.* Livesley Stock and William Dawson resigned as directors and the remaining directors; Robert McKeand, Charles William Baker and Robert Heywood gave notice that they would continue the business as before. Apart from the confusion over Mr Dawson's name, either Patrick or William, it is perhaps significant that some of the directors left the company after only a year or so of operation.

In 1867 the company featured yet again in the 'Bolton Chronicle' when the results of an inquest into a fatal accident were reported. The victim was John Hulse, a labourer in the service of Messrs Mc Kean (sic) and Baker at Turton Moor Colliery. *'At 5.30 in the afternoon of 14 October 1867 Hulse had to hook a rod onto the engine crank to pump water from the pit. He should have waited until the engine stopped but being in a hurry to keep some engagement and it being his time to finish work he tried to accomplish the task with the engine running. He was caught between the crank and the wall and so much injured that he died within half an hour'.* He was 22 years old, unmarried and the son of Samuel Hulse, a butcher of Turton. The verdict was that Hulse had been accidentally killed by machinery.

An article on another accident reported in the 'Bolton Chronicle' in the following year gives a brief insight into colliery routine as follows:-

'About nine-o-clock on Monday morning (21 Dec 1868) the boiler at Turton Moor Colliery, the property of the Turton Moor Coal and Fireclay Company,

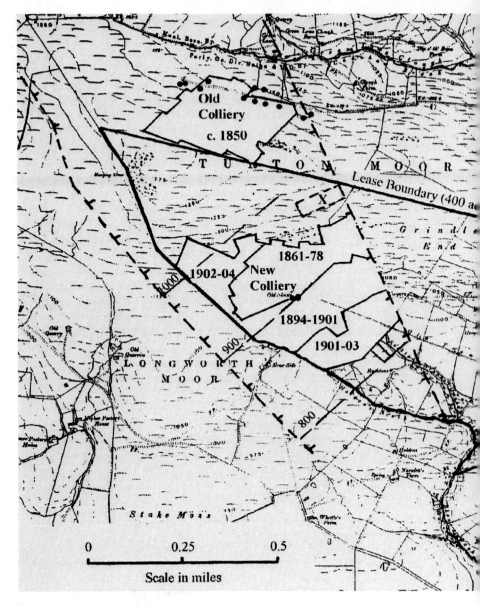

Fig 7. OS map of Turton Moor as it appeared in 1908. Known underground workings un
and 1000 feet above sea level together with the position of major faults, shafts and the fin
supposed to contain dead water in old Turton Moor Colliery – position unknown, probabl

are outlined with dates, approximate levels of the coal seam are shown at 800, 900
boundary. In the area marked 'x' the Inspector of Mines commented- 'Old workings
here.'

situated about 4 miles from Bolton, exploded with terrific violence doing damage amounting to £2000. The boiler was lifted from it's bed and carried a distance of about 25 yards; the engine was turned right over and completely smashed, three brick sheds were hurled to the ground and a chimney about 20 feet high knocked down. Fortunately, however, no lives were lost. The men had started on their way to work, but the weather being most unfavourable and it being pay day, they retraced their steps. Had they been upon the premises at the time of the explosion, it is feared that great loss of life would have ensued. No cause is assigned for the catastrophe. The boiler was nearly new, having been made about two years ago by Messrs Howarth and Cryer of Bolton and the engine at that time was only running at a pressure of 40 lbs which is about 15 lbs less than the pressure at which it was usually worked. It is believed the boiler must have been allowed to get nearly dry, though the man in charge declared there was plenty of water in it.'

To the modern eye it might seem odd that at nine-o'-clock on a Monday morning the men had not yet reported for work, apparently because the weather was bad and it was pay day, yet the reporter seems to find nothing unusual about it. Even the unexplained boiler explosion is treated more as a chance event than evidence that something might be wrong with routine procedures.

When Robert Heywood died in1868, his executors tried to dispose of his share in the company by an auction, advertised in the 'Bolton Chronicle' on 21 January 1871 :-

'Messrs Wm Lomax, Sons and Mills respectfully announce that they are instructed by the trustees under the will of the late Robert Heywood Esq. to offer by public auction on Wednesday 15th February 1871 at five for six o' clock pm, most punctually, at the Three Crowns Inn, Deansgate, Bolton, if not in the meantime disposed of by private treaty, subject to such conditions as shall then be produced.

The leasehold estate and interest of the vendors of and in all that colliery and fire clay works, known as Turton Moor Colliery situated, at Turton, five miles from Bolton, immediately adjoining the turnpike road leading from Bolton to Over Darwen and Blackburn, with the machine house, cart set, tramroad, office, workshops, grinding and drying sheds, chimney and other erections and the whole of the mine or beds of coal and fire clay under 400 statute acres or thereabouts of land at Turton Moor; together with the valuable steam engines for winding, pumping and grinding purposes, with the boiler, shaft fittings, tramways, weighing machine, grinding mill and other machinery and plant in and upon the premises, a schedule of which will be produced at the time of the sale. The colliery is opened out by a winding shaft and an air shaft about 32 (sic) yards in depth, with roadways driven therefrom, and the mines have been proved to be of excellent quality, the produce commanding ready land sale in the district. The colliery is held by lease dated the 16th March 1870 for the unexpired residue of a term of 25 years and three quarters, commencing on the 25th day of December 1867 subject to the yearly footage rent of £50 per foot per Lancashire acre of 7840 square yards for the coal, and an acreage surface rent of £20 per superficial Lancashire acre, irrespective of the thickness for the fire clay, such footage and acreage rent to yield a minimum yearly rent of £150 during the said term, and to the covenants and conditions in the said lease contained. A plan of the workings may be seen and particulars with other information may be had by applying to Mr John Cross, Mining Agent, Cross Street, Manchester; or to Messrs. Rushton and Armistead, solicitors, Bolton, at whose offices a plan of the workings of the mine and a copy of the lease may be seen.'

The list of items is not very different from those disposed of by John Walsh, when he sold the colliery in 1864. It is surprising that the auction did not include any of the kilns for making fireclay products. Mention is made of machinery for grinding the fireclay and a shed for fabricated items to dry out, but of the necessary kilns there is not a word. The lease details are also unusual in that a Lancashire acre of 7 yards to the perch or 7840 sq yds is mentioned rather than of the more usual Cheshire acre of 10240 sq yds or statute acre of 4840 sq yds. The original 15 year lease of 248 acres that started in 1858 must have been renegotiated in 1867, apparently to cover 400 statute acres. However it has been suggested (F. Horridge) that the original 248 acres are Lancashire acres (equivalent to 400 statute acres), in which case the 400 acre lease boundary (Fig 7) seems to have originated in 1858 and persisted in future leases.

The auction resulted in little obvious change and the company continued as a going concern. At least one of the original directors remained because, in the 1871 census, Mr C. W. Baker, is found as a boarder at Parrs Farm, which was close to the main road about half a mile north of Dimple and convenient for the colliery. His occupation is recorded as *'colliery proprietor, fire brick and terra cotta manufacturer, employing 31 men and five boys'* which give a useful indication of the nature and size of the Turton Moor operation at that time.

In the lists of mines for 1866 and 1867 the colliery name is still Turton Moor Colliery and the owners are the Turton Moor Coal Co but in 1868 the name of the colliery itself changes to Turton Moor Brickworks, although the operating company remains the same, presumably the change reflects a new emphasis on fireclay exploitation. This form of entry then persists until 1874 when the operating company becomes Turton Moor Coal and Fireclay Co, there are then no further entries in 1875 or succeeding years. Bolton directories for 1870/1 and 1874 both list Turton Moor Coal and Fire Clay Co. as coal proprietors and fire brick makers located in Egerton, but the are no entries in any later directories.

It can be concluded that virtually the same company worked the colliery from 1865 to 1874 and that from 1866-68 a fireclay works also operated at the site, but by 1875 all commercial operations seem to have ended. Finally in 1878 an abandonment plan was submitted with details of all workings since the time of Briggs and Walsh, but without any indication of the older workings, by Andrew Knowles, on the other side of the hill. The owners of the mine who submitted the plan were the executors of R Heywood, which suggests that Robert Heywood's share in the company might not have been disposed of after all. Heywood's executors had considerable discretion over the management of assets and if the 1871 auction failed to produce an acceptable bid, they probably decided to continue their interest in the company.

The production of fireclay at the site is particularly interesting. A substantial thickness of good quality fireclay is associated with the Lower Mountain Mine and it is not surprising that the company should try to exploit it. At this colliery there were 8-9 feet of fireclay separating a 'bottom coal', 18-20 inches thick and a 'top coal' 6-8 inches thick (which may not have been worth working) (Fig 8). Fireclay was used to make heat resistant bricks to line industrial furnaces, firebricks for simple domestic fireplaces, acid resisting ware, terra-cotta, glazed bricks and electric cable conduits. Also because fireclay is quite pliable, it could be easily worked and even extruded, to form sewage pipes and the other items of what is called sanitary ware.

It is probable that, as Turton Moor Colliery became less competitive in the local market for coal, it would increasingly turn to fireclay products to remain viable, using coal from the mine for firing its kilns. Several local fireclay producers once worked in this way. Two mines existed until the 1960s, Adam Mason and Sons at Montcliffe and Crankshaws at Wildersmoor. While at Darwen, in the early part of the twentieth century, the Lower Mountain Mine was worked for coal and fireclay in mines near Cranberry Fold, at Taylor's Green and in a large operation at Hoddlesden. With the demise of domestic coal fires and more intense conditions in industrial furnaces, use of fireclay products has declined over the last half century. The demand is now satisfied from opencast coal workings and deposits in Lancashire that were once worked underground are now of little value.

The new colliery shaft, on the south side of Turton Moor, was fairly central to the area underlain by the coal seam but not at a place where it came particularly near to the surface and the amount of sinking might be minimised. Perhaps there were good reasons for selecting this particular spot for the shaft, but it resulted in the pit being rather inconveniently located, at a high altitude on the side of the moor, where a long tramway was needed to connect with the main road.

Two shafts close together would have been provided from an early date. They were located at an altitude of about 1070 feet and went to a depth of 174 feet so the seam at the shaft bottom was at an elevation of about 900 feet above sea level (Figs 7, 8 & 9). Drainage would have been a problem and it is significant that a pump was always present when equipment was auctioned. The pump would not have raised water to the surface but more likely connected to a tunnel with a shallow gradient that discharged into a nearby valley. A tunnel entrance, now obscured, is shown on the geological map alongside Holden Brook, at an elevation of 940 feet. Use of this tunnel, about 2000 feet long, would allow the shaft bottom to be drained by raising the water through a vertical distance of about 40 feet rather than to the top of the shaft. This tunnel, or one like it, was possibly the subject of the dispute in 1865 involving the gradient, which would, of course, be absolutely critical for effective drainage.

Once down the shafts mining proceeded towards the rise of the seam, that is to say towards the northwest and the old working of Andrew Knowles (Fig 7). This arrangement allowed the products to be easily transported down gradient, back to the pit bottom for winding to the surface. Also water would run back into a sump, where the pump could handle it. The working would be by pillar and stall, the traditional method of mining in Lancashire. By later standards the exploitation was fairly modest and working did not advance more than 1000 feet up the rise while on either side it was constrained by large faults and the lease boundary. At the limits of the working on the rise side, the mine plan shows that small faults were increasingly encountered and the strata were becoming contorted. These structural problems and the fear of encountering old workings probably curtailed further progress.

As the sales potential of fireclay, as a raw material, would always have been rather restricted, the company, like most other fireclay producers, set up a fabricating plant and kilns for firing the product near to their mine. At Turton Moor these were erected immediately next to the colliery where buildings that look like kilns and other accommodation for making fireclay articles are in evidence on the plan (Fig 9). A spoil heap, that can still be inspected, is found adjacent to the site of the kilns. It is composed almost entirely of waste fired articles made from fireclay and confirms that manufacturing occurred here.

In 1875, as mining activities were running down, one last accident was reported in the 'Bolton Journal' on 26 June 1875 when Edward Ward of Over Darwen, aged 14, was killed by a roof fall at the colliery as he was removing a tub of coal. Some underground exploration and a little extraction seems to have continued until 1878, after which the colliery was formally abandoned and a plan of the final workings submitted to the Inspector of Mines. The Inspector, at that time the respected Mr Dickinson, signed the document to show that he was satisfied with it and indicated an approximate position where Andrew Knowles's old workings were thought to be and included a written warning that these were supposed to contain 'dead water' (Fig 7). Presumably, even in 1878, knowledge of the old colliery, closed 23 years earlier, was very limited.

Whether the old workings posed a real threat is not clear. If the old drainage was entirely by gravity and the water channels had remained open, then the workings should have remained dry, but perhaps Mr Dickinson had some information to the contrary. Certainly Knowles's workings were at a higher level than those of the new colliery and any accidental contact between the two would be dangerous if there was any standing water.

After the colliery was abandoned, all the surface plant and the tramway were removed, so that, on the OS map of 1894, not even the path of the tramway is marked and all that remains at the pit head is one small square structure with a side about 15 feet long that might be a protective structure around a shaft (Fig 9). Alongside the main road, where the later pipe works was to be established, there were no recognisable structures at all. After pumping stopped, the workings would soon become flooded, at least up to the level of the drainage tunnel and eventually the whole colliery would become derelict.

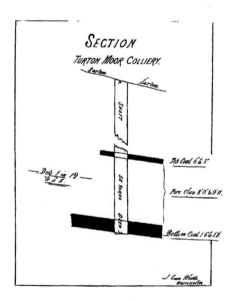

Fig 8. ..Shaft section from the mine plan of 1878, showing the inclination of the strata, depth of shaft and thickness of coal and fireclay.

36

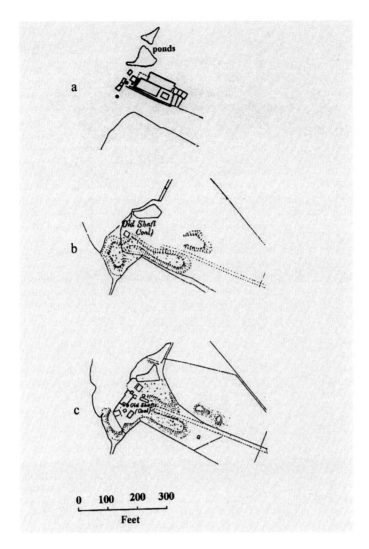

Fig 9   Plans showing surface features at the new colliery between 1878 and 1910.

Top (a): Shafts, tramway and brickworks of the Turton Moor Coal and Fireclay Co from the mine plan of 1878.

Middle (b): Spoil heaps and a small structure, probably covering a shaft, on an otherwise derelict pit head site from the 1:2500 OS map of 1894.

Lower (c): Pit head facilities of Darwen Sanitary Pipe Ltd after closure in 1905 and lifting of the tramway, from the 1:2500 OS map of 1910.

One of the shafts at the new colliery, the other in the background. The shaft, capped with concrete, is obscured by debris and grass.

Detail of one of the low walls surrounding the shafts, showing the use of stone, brick and blocks made from fireclay. All the fabricated items would have been made on site by the Turton Moor Coal and Fireclay Co or at the post 1893 pipe works.

The ruins of Coopers Farm, one of the few with walls left standing. The colliery and Turton Moor are in the background.

Fireclay blocks in a section of wall at Coopers. The farm obviously used such articles for building when the opportunity offered.

Chapter 7   TURTON MOOR SANITARY PIPE CO. & DARWEN SANITARY PIPES LTD.

In 1893, after 15 years of idleness, the colliery was reopened, this time by the Turton Moor Sanitary Pipe Company. The original shafts were brought back into operation and a new tramway was installed to connect the colliery to a pipe works constructed on Charters Moss, near the main highway (Figs 10 & 11).

The demand for fireclay pipes had increased significantly when public health legislation, in the 19th century, required local authorities to construct sewage systems on a large scale. Fireclay, on account of its plasticity, was an ideal material from which to make the salt glazed pipes that, until the last forty years or so, were the mainstay of domestic sewage systems. The last phase of activity at the colliery was mainly to serve this market.

The company mined coal and fireclay, raised the products to the surface in separate tubs then ran the tubs down the tramway to the pipe works. It was usual to leave the fireclay on a stockpile for a year or so to weather, which made it easier to work and allowed impurities to be removed. The fireclay would then be ground with a limited amount of water until it reached the necessary consistency, then fabricated into the usual pipe shape and be fired in batches in the kilns.

Local directories at this time record the existence of the company. In the four Post Office Directories for Bolton that cover the years between 1894 and 1904, the Turton Moor Sanitary Pipe, Firebrick and Clay Co Ltd is listed with Charters Moss, Egerton as its location. In one entry even the name of the company secretary (James Fish) is recorded.

In 1901 the company changed its name to the Darwen Sanitary Pipes Ltd. (Fig 12), although to an outsider little else seemed to have changed, in that there was no period of idleness between owners, the colliery manager retained his job and the number of men employed remained much the same. The Post Office Directory for Bolton never even acknowledged the change and continued to list the operation as the 'Turton Moor Sanitary Pipe, Fire-brick and Clay Co. Ltd.'- even in the 1902-1904 issue. Barret's Directory for Blackburn did a little better by referring, in its 1906 issue, to 'Turton Moor (Darwen) Sanitary Pipe Co'.

Company records show that the Turton Moor Sanitary Pipe Co Ltd was established in December 1893. There were originally 17 shareholders holding a total of 89 shares. They were nearly all from Darwen or Blackburn, which is not so surprising as the mining of fireclay and manufacture of fireclay articles was a well established industry in Darwen at this time, whereas in Turton there was never anything comparable and even in Bolton it was only a minor business.

The terms of reference of the new company allowed it to acquire and mine coal, fireclay and other minerals in a 400 acre lease on Turton Moor (Fig 7) and to make sanitary and drain pipes, and other fireclay and earthenware products. In addition it could acquire warehouses, workshops, factories, houses, railways and tramways etc.

The lease was acquired by means of an indenture, dated 22 June 1894, between the Lord of the Manor of Turton (Peter A. M. Hoare) and two directors of the company, Jeshurun L Coulthurst and William Taylor. This gave the company liberty to *'sink pit shafts, make levels, drifts, soughs, tunnels, airways and watercourses, as necessary, for getting, selling and carrying away coal and fireclay'*. It also allowed the construction of reservoirs and use of any water in the lease area for mining, brick and pipe making and for steam engines, steam boilers and condensing purposes. The company was at liberty to erect houses, smithies, workshops, sheds, gins, fire engines, ovens and other buildings and machinery. It could get stone, set out roads and store stone or deposit rubbish on the land.

The company went ahead with its remit, erected the pipe works, set out the tramway and brought the old shafts back into operation, although it would probably be well into 1894 before the venture became fully operational. It soon became an important producer in the area and the Turton local authority was included among its customers. Unfortunately the period of financial viability was short lived, if it ever really existed, for at an extraordinary general meeting on 7 November 1900, notice was given of the shareholders decision to wind up the company, as the liabilities were thought to be too great, and a liquidator was appointed. Prior to this there had been further calls for capital and the number of shareholders had increased, all of them from much the same geographic location as previously with the exception of Dr James Robinson, a medical practitioner of 'Rockfield' Dunscar and one time Medical Officer of Health for Turton.

The liquidator intended to auction the business and advertised in the 'Darwen News' in February 1901 as follows:-

'To be sold by auction at the Millstone Hotel, Darwen on 28 February 1901.

All the business and undertaking ...carried on by the Turton Moor Sanitary Pipe Co Ltd at Turton Moor, near Bolton as sanitary pipe and plastic brick manufacturer and colliery proprietors with goodwill and motive power, gearing, shafting, piping and machinery and loose plant and tools and effects not being stock in trade, together with a lease of the valuable mines of coal and fireclay lying under 400 acres of land at Turton Moor. The lease is for 28 and a quarter years from June 1893 with an option for breaking at the end of the 18th year.'

Further details and a schedule of the plant were to be obtained from, among others, Mr James Cocker, Bolton Road, Darwen (the liquidator) or Mr Charles Costaker of Darwen (the company solicitor).

The firm was rescued, apparently at the last minute, by a group of the shareholders who set up a new company to take over the assets and debts and continue the Turton Moor operation as a going concern. A formal agreement to this effect was made between James Cocker and Arthur Longworth on 28 February 1901. At the time the financial position and value of the acquisition, to the nearest pound, was as follows:-

	£
Pottery and colliery at Turton Moor	5100
Book debts	5009
Stocks	2798
Expenses	95
Bank balance	748
Total	**13750**

As a final part of the transfer process, notices were placed in the 'Darwen News' on 16 and 23 March 1901 by the company solicitor requiring creditors of the Turton Moor Sanitary Pipe Co. Ltd. to notify James Cocker, of their address and particulars of their debt by 1 June 1901, or they would be excluded from the benefits of the company sale.

The new company came into official existence on 16 March 1901. On its headed notepaper, it styled itself Darwen Sanitary Pipes Limited, Darwen and had the telegram address Pipes, Darwen, yet the registered office remained at Turton Moor, its railway traffic still went through Bromley Cross and all its assets seem to have been located in Turton, only the ownership remained firmly rooted in Darwen. Perhaps too much association with Turton Moor somehow detracted from the sense of dynamism conferred by a Darwen address. The new company was obviously very proud of its acquisition and designed a very fine letter head bearing a picture of the pipe works and a list of the main products, including sanitary pipes from 3 inch up to 42 inch in diameter, water closets, chimney tops, glazed earthenware sinks, farm animal troughs and firebricks etc. The company trade mark was a pipe marked 42 inches diameter, the largest they made, which was probably recognised as being difficult to fabricate and therefore indicative of an advanced pipe making facility.

The physical assets of the new company were much the same as previously; that is to say, coal, fireclay and other minerals under 400 acres of land at Turton Moor with offices, sheds, smithies, store rooms, engine and boiler houses, mechanics house and shop, grinding rooms, brick drying shed, moulding rooms and other buildings; also kilns, chimneys, engines, boilers, motive power, gearing, plant, machinery, fixtures etc.,

Unfortunately, the Darwen company did not have any more commercial success than its predecessor and on 12 July 1911 there was yet another extraordinary general meeting of the shareholders when it was agreed that a liquidator be appointed to wind up the company. Subsequently matters progressed rapidly and on 13 December 1911 the Darwen Sanitary pipe company officially ceased to exist. At the end the assets, to nearest pound, were listed as follows:-

	£
Pottery, colliery plant, expenditure on sinking new shaft	1062
Horses and lorries	72
Stock, pipes etc at cost	838
Cash at bank	390
Cash in hand	6

The letterhead used by the Darwen company gives an impression of how the works looked in its heyday, probably about 1901 (Fig 10 & 12). It was fashionable at that time to show company premises in promotional literature and although perspectives might be altered to make buildings seem more grand, the illustration of the pipe works is the only one available and is otherwise quite instructive. In the foreground is the main road from Bolton to Darwen and in the background is Turton Moor itself with a faint impression of the tramway running up to the colliery. The pipe works site consists of a stocking area on the right where piles of fireclay are being left to weather, then there are 16 kilns visible (compared with 14 on the OS map), 6 chimneys and several substantial buildings. There is a notable absence of any domestic housing, although the company seems to have had power to provide it, but probably the finances were never strong enough.

The new colliery would have a difficulty from the outset, in that, by taking over an old working, they had to make do with coal and fireclay that the previous operation had taken no interest in. The earlier operation had ensured that all workings were on the raise side of the shafts so that underground transport of mine products and drainage could be by gravity alone. Apart from an area near the western boundary fault, all the post-1893 workings followed the seam downwards, below the level of the shafts leaving the products to be hauled back up a 1 in 14 gradient to the pit bottom. Water would also have to be brought up to the pit bottom from where it could be pumped to the surface and additional pumping capacity would be needed. As mining progressed to deeper levels, further from the shaft, the complexity of the operation would inevitably increase.

Unfortunately, one of the lateral limits to the workings, is formed by a fault and the other by a lease boundary, converging down dip so that the amount of coal available for extraction at each level becomes progressively reduced and, had extraction proceeded far enough, this factor alone could have put and end to the mine. However the mining plan indicates the possible presence of a further fault, near Rushtons farm (Fig 7) that cuts out the coal, so that the opportunity for further mining would have been even more limited.

One of the best records of this period is the 1:2500 Ordnance Survey map published in 1910. Here the pipe works on Charter's Moss is shown very clearly (Fig 11) together with the route of the tramway up the hillside to the colliery. The map was surveyed in 1908, soon after the mine closed, but all the pit-head buildings still seem to be standing although the shafts must have been idle (Fig 9). The course of the tramway is shown, marked "Old Tramway", but the actual track seems to have been lifted. No indication is given on the map as to the operational state of the pipe works and it could still have been active.

It is not very clear how events unfolded towards the end of the life of the Darwen company, but even by 1905 things seemed to be going downhill. The list issued by the Inspector of Mines notes that the colliery was 'discontinued' in 1906, then seems to have been reactivated in 1907, then 'discontinued' again in 1908, apparently permanently, although it was never described as abandoned which is usual when a colliery is finally closed. Clearly the number of people employed at the colliery after 1905 was so small that, whether discontinued or not, it could not have maintained an output sufficient to satisfy the original pipe works or to provide much traffic for the tramway.

One pointer as to the state of affairs at the works is provided by a report from the Sanitary Inspector to Turton Council in April 1905 which is headed *Turton Moor Pipe Works – Re Salt Fumes*, and reads as follows:- *'I called at these works on 12 April and interviewed the manager as to the abatement of the nuisance. He said in future he would arrange that only one kiln instead of three would be finishing at a time. He also informed me that by the end of this week the whole of the kilns would close down for an indefinite period, but on resumption of work the above arrangement will be carried out from which time I will keep the same under observation and report.'* There do not seem to have been any further reports, perhaps they never became necessary. In any case the promise of closure for an indefinite period sounds ominous and otherwise the run down in activity seems to start about this time. The reference to *'kilns finishing'* probably refers to a final stage in the process when salt was introduced to form the glaze.

In 1905 payment of rates was an issue for the company as on 2 May, apparently for the first time, they had to be reminded to pay their Poor Rate of £90-6s-3d.

The company tried to get their assessment reduced but were met with the reply from Turton Council. - *'I cannot see how we can allow you anything off the rate seeing that men are employed on the premises. I shall esteem it a favour if you will kindly let me have a payment of the rate by 30th inst. and oblige.'* But the local authority eventually relented and in the following year the company received a repayment of £37-11s-0d on account of *'the assessment having been reduced during the currency of the rate'*. The quest for a rate reduction continued and on 21 Nov 1907 Turton Council wrote, *'I notice from the last list of appeals received from the assessment committee that you did not appear before them re your appeal against the revised assessment of the kiln at the Turton Moor Pipe Works. This being the case I must ask you to kindly let me have payment by Monday next as the rates are now overdue'*. On 22 July 1909 there was yet another appeal when the local authority wrote – *'I enclose a demand note showing the amount of rates due from you. I have no doubt you are aware the assessment committee has postponed your appeal until February 1910 and that they have ordered me to charge you on £100 rateable value pending such settlement. The enclosed demand notes show the amount due according to such decision. Will you kindly let me have a cheque for the same by next Wednesday. If you cannot manage the other please let me have payment of the District rate'*.

Obviously the company thought the rates should be reduced in line with scaled down industrial activity. By 1907 there is a suggestion that only one kiln was operational and the colliery would have produced very little in that year. Turton Council was fairly sympathetic, recognising, at least in 1909, that the company might have difficulty making the payment. Finally on 6 Oct 1911, just a few weeks before the closure, a glimpse of the state of things at the pipe works is given in the following letter from Turton Council – *'I herewith return the demand notes showing the amount of rates due on the mine and works at Charters Moss. No doubt the Assessment Committee had in mind the fact of your premises becoming empty, hence the very low assessment thereof. I am sorry I cannot allow you exemption on the said premises as when I visited last Tuesday, I noticed the place was stocked with pipes and the colliery head with machinery which had been there for sometime.'*

On the northern edge of the pipe-works site the OS map of 1908 shows another shaft marked 'Old Shaft (Coal)' (Fig 11), that was definitely sunk after 1893. Its purpose is not obvious but it might well be the site of colliery head referred to in the letter from the local authority although once again there are no mine plans available to make matters clear. A new shaft is referred to in the 1911 assessment of the value of the company in a way that suggests it was still regarded as an asset and Mike Rothwell reports that a shaft was sunk in 1907 but gives no further details. The sinking of this shaft after the mine had closed could explain the curious reactivation of the colliery in 1907 reported by the Inspector of Mines.

A seam of fireclay and coal known as Sand Rock Mine is thought to exist under the site and although it has never been worth working in Turton, it had been mined extensively on Winter Hill. If the new shaft was intended to exploit this seam as a separate colliery, at this date, there should be another, independent means of underground access, but there is no sign of it, nor is there any indication of what was to be done about drainage. Alternatively if the new shaft was to link with the existing workings it is possible to speculate about other uses. Whatever the real intention, the new shaft seems to have been something of a forlorn hope, although after the main colliery closed, it seemed to persist for a time, without producing anything of significance, as if it was expected that a reopening might eventually occur.

The mine certainly did not die through lack of exploration activity as several boreholes were put down over the lease area to test the location and reserves of the coal seam and evaluate the rest of the lease. These did not give encouraging results and showed little scope for further extraction outside the recognised 'coalfield'.

Under legislation dating from 1872 every mine, on closing, was required to deposit a plan of workings with the Inspector of Mines. Inspectors were assiduous in collecting such plans, known as Abandonment Plans, and prosecution was threatened for any coal owner who did not comply. Deposition of these plans is still required and the collection is maintained by the Coal Authority. A plan showing the state of the workings when the Turton Moor Coal and Fireclay Co abandoned them in 1878, is available and has already been mentioned, but there is no corresponding abandonment plan that covers the last stage of working by the Darwen Sanitary Pipe Co., which ought to have been made sometime between 1906 and 1911. Not only is the plan absent from the official collection, but it never seems to have been deposited in the first place. This curious situation perhaps confirms that the colliery was expected eventually to reopen, although it still does not explain why the apparent lapse was overlooked by the authorities. Fortuitously at the Manchester Museum of Science and Industry a plan does exist, made in 1906, when the usual colliery operations were near to ending, if they had not already done so. All our knowledge about underground workings after 1893 are based on this plan which unfortunately includes nothing about the 'new shaft'.

Fig 10   View of pipe works, circa 1901, enlarged from company letterhead.

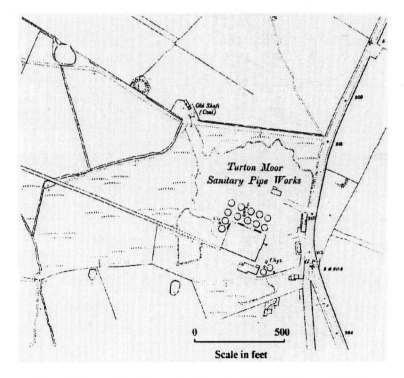

Fig 11   Plan of the pipe works from the 1:2500 OS map of 1910.

47

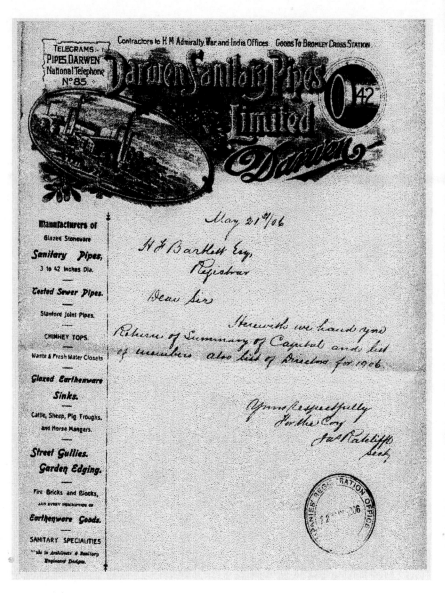

Fig 12   Headed paper of Darwen Sanitary Pipes Limited.

The remains of Moor Side Farm in Longworth with spoil heaps at the new colliery in the background. John Riley a 'fireman at the brickworks' lodged here in 1871, no doubt to be close to the 'brickworks', which were then alongside the colliery.

Another view of a capped shaft. Presumably the shaft was made safe and walled round by Darwen Sanitary Pipes Ltd after 1905 and before the company was finally wound up in 1911.

Line of the tramway as it approaches the colliery.

A surviving rail on the trackbed of the tramway

Sanitary pipes on Turton Moor near the pipe works.

The insignia of the Turton Moor Sanitary Pipe Co. on the above pipes.
The company ceased to exist in 1901.

The site of Rushtons Farm with colliery spoil heaps in the distance. This point is at the furthest extent of the workings where they would be about 170 feet deep. In 1901 two colliers resided here, John Burns, head of the household, and John Kirkman, lodger. In 1871 Samuel Crook, a 'steam engine driver' lived here and would have been employed at Turton Moor.

Remains of the shaft near the pipe works. This was the last shaft to be sunk, probably as part of a final effort to save the company.

Chapter 8   PEOPLE

None of the people involved in the mining activities at Turton Moor are now alive. Even if they were, they might not want to be reminded about time and money spent on operations that lacked any long term success, but before leaving them, it is worth taking a closer look at the individuals concerned, where they lived and what sort of work they did. For the most part the relevant data comes from census returns corresponding to the different phases of activity, that is to say 1901, 1871 and 1851 and from remaining company records, newspapers and official mining records.

In 1894 the Inspector of Mines began to publish an annual record of the number of men at each colliery. For this purpose, at Turton Moor, the colliery would be regarded as a separate entity from the pipe works. The number of men employed, names of the managers and under managers and the operational status of the colliery were recorded as follows:-

Date	Manager	Under Manager	Men employed		Notes
			underground	surface	
1893	William Taylor	-	n.d.	n.d.	
1894	William Taylor	-	43	16	
1895	William Taylor	Jonathan Taylor	51	9	
1896	William Taylor	Jonathan Taylor	60	10	
1897	William Taylor	Jonathan Taylor	74	14	
1898	Joseph Miller	Jonathan Taylor	65	14	
1899	William Taylor	Jonathan Taylor	80	15	
1900	William Taylor	-	72	12	
1901	William Taylor	John Thos. Taylor	62	17	
1902	William Taylor	John Thos. Taylor	73	15	
1903	William Taylor	John Thos. Taylor	50	13	
1904	John Thos. Taylor	-	60	12	
1905	John Thos. Taylor	-	30	5	
1906	John Thos. Taylor	-	19	-	discontinued
1907	John Thos. Taylor	-	7	3	
1908	-	-	-	-	discontinued
1909	-	-	-	-	discontinued

The Taylor family is obviously strongly represented in management. William Taylor (b 1837), the original mine manager and a shareholder, was eventually succeeded by his son John Thomas Taylor (b 1875). They are found in the census return of 1881 when the family lived at 44 Watery Lane, Darwen and William Taylor recorded his profession as 'Colliery Manager, Mine Service'. When the Turton Moor Sanitary Pipe Company was first established in 1893 he was living in Hoddlesden, but by 1901 had moved to 51 Park Road, Darwen, which is on the west side of Bolton Road almost opposite the junction with Watery Lane, not far from one of his previous homes. The house, which still stands, was then on the fringe of the town, well placed for the long walk over the hill to Turton Moor, which must have been William Taylor's lot every time he went to the colliery. Nor would he have been the only one, for Joseph Miller, manager in 1898, was a neighbour at 57 Park Road, while Jonathan Taylor (b 1862), the under manager until 1898, lived nearby at 56 Cemetery Road with a son, also employed at the pipe works. In 1903, William Taylor finally ceased to be the manager, he was 66 and no doubt old enough for a well deserved retirement.

At that time hundreds of people in Darwen were employed in several local pipeworks or collieries and mostly they worked near to home. However there is no doubt that some were prepared to walk from Darwen to Turton Moor to work, but most of the individuals concerned are impossible to identify.

Conversely in nearby parts of Turton there were no other collieries or pipe works that were at all accessible and it can be assumed, with some confidence, that all the colliers and pipe makers, living around Egerton and recorded in the census, worked at Turton Moor.

The 1901 census returns covering relevant parts of Turton show that 33 people worked at a sanitary pipe works (presumably Turton Moor) and a further 21 were colliery workers, of which 19 worked underground. On the other hand the Inspector of Mines records 62 men working underground at Turton Moor in 1901 and although the two sets of figures might not be expected to balance exactly, it is clear that most of the colliers at Turton Moor did not live in Turton. The only other likely place would be Darwen and it must be assumed that most of the remainder must have walked from here over Bull Hill to work each day, with a few perhaps coming from isolated farms or cottages

If the proportion of colliers to pipe makers found in the Turton census is typical, then the 79 men recorded by the Inspector of Mines as working at the colliery should be matched by a further 124 or so at the pipe works, making a total labour force of 203. Even if the figures are not very accurate, there can be little doubt that the Turton Moor company was a substantial employer and its early closure must have caused some disruption and disappointment in the area.

The residences of colliers and sanitary pipe workers in Turton, within range of Turton Moor, according to the 1901 census, were mainly in Egerton, more specifically in cottages along Blackburn Road, at Dimple, Egerton Vale, Longworth Road, Union Road, Bright Street, Bedford Street and Warburton Fold. A few others lived or lodged at convenient farms including Knowles, Rushtons, Ramsdens, Yates, Butterworths, Tewit, Buffs and in some cottages adjacent to Green Arms Inn.

In December 1893 when the Turton Moor Sanitary Pipe Co Ltd was established there were 17 shareholders including directors, but by 1898 the number had increased to 29. The list confirms the Darwen orientation of the owners and it is noteworthy that, among the founding shareholders, not a single one came from Turton or Bolton, even by 1898 when the list had expanded, there was only Dr James Robinson from Turton.

Among the shareholders, William Taylor, the first colliery manager, has already been mentioned together with Jeshurun Coulthurst who negotiated the lease with the landowner. Otherwise the initial importance of Fred Baynes as the major shareholder may be noted. After the reorganisation in 1901 many shareholders withdrew, leaving a new company in fewer and perhaps more optimistic hands. Details of the shareholders over the years are given in the accompanying table.

In the previous period of activity from 1862 to1876 the labour force was much smaller. The operating company only employed 8 colliers in 1862 and the census return for one of the directors (Mr Baker) shows that only 36 men and boys were employed in 1871. A difficulty with the 1871 census is that it does not describe some occupations very precisely. For example, in 1871 fireclay works are frequently referred to simply as 'brickworks' whereas in 1891 they would more typically have been described as 'sanitary pipe works', consequently less confidence can be placed in identifying people who might be employed in the works at Turton Moor. Fortunately the same problem does not extend to colliers working underground and even with colliery surface workers the connection with mining is usually made clear. For these reasons, in addition to the usual difficulties in matching two sets of statistics, it would be too much to expect all the people who worked for Mr Baker to be identifiable in the census return, but enough of them can be found to make the exercise worthwhile.

The situation at Turton in 1871 was complicated by the presence of several other collieries and allowance has to be made for the colliery and fireclay works on Winter Hill, which probably gave employment to people in Belmont, while a similar industry on Cranberry Moss probably accounted for most of those in Entwistle. There was also a small colliery at Horrocks Court that could conveniently have employed colliers from Chapeltown or Overhouses. However, even allowing for the alternative places of employment, the colliers and others living around Egerton seem numerous enough to make up the bulk of the labour force at Turton Moor colliery. Some others must have come from Darwen, Edward Ward (killed in the accident in 1875) certainly did, but there were probably not many like him.

Turning now to the details of the 1871 census it is probably significant that John Riley lodged at Moor Side Farm, close to the colliery. His job was to keep the kilns fired and as they would operate on a 24 hour basis he would find it

Shareholders in the Turton Moor Sanitary Pipe Co. (1893-1901) and Darwen Sanitary Pipes Ltd. (1900-1911)

Name	Residence	Occupation	Number of shares		
			1893	1898	19
John Isherwood	Pleasington	paper manufacturer	5	-	-
John K Adcroft	13 Salford, Blackburn	milliner	5	-	-
Jes. L Coulthurst	51 Blackburn Rd. Darwen	ironfounder	5	12	1(
William Taylor	Rock Villa, Hoddlesden (1893) 51 Park Rd. Darwen (1898)	colliery manager	5	3	-
Geo. Ollerenshaw	Cherry Tree, Blackburn	tea merchant	5	5	
George Adcroft	152 Shear Brow, Blackburn	merchant	5	-	-
Charles Costeker	4 Church St. Darwen (1893-8) The Willows, Lytham (1911)	solicitor	5	10	1(
William Stubbs	2 Bank St. Darwen (1893) 100 Preston N. Rd. Blackburn	borough surveyor	5	3	1(
John Titherington	63 Stopes Brow, L. Darwen	draper	3	3	-
James Cocker	Bolton Rd. Darwen (1893) Park Rd. Darwen (1898) Inglewood, Darwen (1911)	builder & contractor	5	5	2(
William T Gent	Weir St. Blackburn	cotton waste dealer	3	-	-
John Rutherford	Salford New Brewery, Blackburn	brewer	5	-	-
Fred Baynes	Cicely Bridge Mill, Blackburn	cotton spinner	20	10	-
Arthur Longworth	Whalley	cotton manufacturer	2	9	2(
Wm B Huntington	Woodlands, Darwen	paper maker	5	-	-
Thos. Thompson	121 Westgate, Burnley	herbalist	3	5	-
Mark T Jepson	Hindle St. Darwen (1893) 24 Epworth St. Darwen	gentleman	1	4	5(
George Hopkins	19 St James St. Burnley	draper	-	2	-
Timothy Y Nutall	Parkside, Darwen	paper manufacturer	-	2	-
Sarah J Goodall	95 Sussex Rd. Southport	lady	-	4	-
R. M. Bottomly	King St. Blackburn	taylor	-	2	-
Thomas Atherton	15 Bull Hill, Darwen	gentleman	-	2	2;
James Robinson	Rockfield, Dunscar	medical doctor	-	5	5(
John Scott	Easter tyne Ho. Ballingling NB	agent	-	5	-
Rev. G Greenway	Darwen Bank, Blackburn	gentleman	-	5	-
Moses Duxbury	Valemount, Darwen	paper mill manager	-	5	2(
Mathew Shaw	13 Juke Thomas St. Blackburn	gentleman	-	5	-
Marg. Ainsworth	Hollins Lane, Darwen	grocer	-	1	-
Thomas A Eccles	Grange, Darwen	cotton manufacturer	-	3	-
W.T Sharples	West View, Wilpshire	agent	-	5	-
Jas. T Ballantyne	Holker House, Darwen	medical doctor	-	4	-
William Entwistle	Rose Hill Villa, Darwen	stone merchant	-	5	-
Joshua Hacking	Enfield Ho. Clayton-le-Moors	soap manufacturer	-	10	-
James Hacking	Enfield Ho. Clayton-le-Moors	soap manufacturer	-	5	-
Bryan L Holme	61 Belgrave, Darwen	solicitor	-	10	-
Dr C Baynes	135 Revidge Rd. Blackburn	esquire	-	-	10
T hos. W Crook	-	-	-	-	25
J Cooper	-	-	-	-	25

Names in bold are of Turton Moor Company shareholders, including some founders from 1893, who persisted with their holdings under the Darwen Company, among these A. Longworth, M. Duxbury, J. Cocker, C Baynes and M. T. Jepson were directors in 1911.

Items marked * in the 1911 column indicate share ownership by executors following an earlier death.

Dimple in 1963 from Blackburn Road: other than isolated farms and cottages, Dimple provided the nearest housing to Turton Moor. In 1871 Thomas Lawton, a collier lived at No 12 Dimple while James Kay, a brickworks labourer lived at No 27. In 1901 Charles J Walsh was at No 3 and James Southern at No 41, both were colliers.

Cottages at Dimple c. 1935.

Longworth Road, Egerton: in 1901 three of these houses were occupied by people working at Turton Moor as follows:- No2, William Lee, collier; No4, William T Patrick, sanitary moulder; No 28, John Ward, banksman at coal pit and Andrew Ward, collier.

Egerton Vale: in 1901 three of these cottages were occupied by colliers:- No 1, James Knight; No 4, Harry Heap; No 6 Robert W Sayer.

Cottages at Union Street, Egerton: in 1901 Charles A Rigby a 'sanitary pipe maker' lived at No 14.

Moss Cottage, between Dimple and Turton Moor: one of the nearest structures to Turton Moor still standing. In 1871, Samuel Briggs and James Crook, both 'colliery engine drivers' lived here.

Park Road, Darwen: William Taylor, manager of Turton Moor Colliery, 1893-1903, and company shareholder lived at the end house.

Joseph Dickinson (1818-1912): one of the first of the HM Inspector of Mines. He served from 1850 until 1892, and was mainly concerned with collieries in the Manchester area. His comments are recorded on the Turton Moor abandonment plan of 1878.

convenient to live in the nearest possible habitation. Otherwise the presence of no less than three steam engine drivers, two at Moss Cottage and one at Rushtons, suggests that there may have been several engines or that some of the machinery, perhaps the pumps, required drivers working in shifts. Other nearby farms housing colliers or people working at the brickworks included Platts, Whewells and Parrs (where the director C.W.Baker lodged). Otherwise the labour force mostly occupied cottages at Green Arms, Dimple and Egerton.

John Walsh of Briggs and Walsh, who started the new colliery in 1862, lived at Grainings which is on Bolton Road on the Darwen side of Bull Hill. The company which took over from him in 1864, Turton Moor Coal (and Fireclay) Co started with five shareholders, Livesely Stock, William Dawson, Richard Barnes, Robert McKeand, Charles Baker and Robert Heywood, but by 1866 only Robert Mc Keand, Charles Baker and Robert Heywood remained. Robert Heywood (1786-1868) of Bolton is well known and was twice mayor of the town, a prominent Unitarian and cotton manufacturer. After his death in 1868 his executors seem to have retained an interest until the company was wound up and in the final years may have been the sole owners.

If the 10 men mentioned in the rating assessment of 1849 reflect the longer term employment position, then there should not be many colliers to account for at Turton Moor in the 1851 census. Unfortunately the situation is complicated by the usual presence of other collieries nearby, including Old Lyons and Dogshaw collieries, just over the boundary in Darwen and the workings on Winter Hill and, Entwistle Moss.

The miners living nearest to Turton Moor include Thomas Fish, aged 32, who was later killed in an accident at Turton Moor colliery and is listed as a coal miner and head of a household that included his wife and 3 children at Moor House (near Whewells Farm) on Turton Moor. Otherwise Jonas Crook of Lower Barn (near Coopers Farm) seems to have been the colliery banksman, while Mark Ward at Moorside in Longworth and William Taylor of Cabbage Row (opposite the Cross Guns Inn) probably also worked at Turton Moor. All the others, listed in the surrounding area, would have found it more convenient to work in one of the other collieries although this does not necessarily mean they did so. Perhaps a few walked to Turton Moor to work, but there is no means of identifying them.

Before leaving the colliers listed in the census returns it is worth noting the strong persistence of certain family names such as Fish, Almond and Harwood, showing that mining, in this area, like many others, tended to be a family occupation in which sons followed fathers.

61

Chapter 9   EPILOGUE

Looking back on the 66 years of intermittent mining at Turton Moor, the most lasting impression is of the optimism of those who tried to exploit this small, remote and economically marginal mineral deposit.

First Andrew Knowles employed about 10 men to produce coal from some shallow workings from the mid 1840s to 1855, before leaving the area for ever. Then in 1862 Briggs and Walsh developed a new colliery, probably at considerable expense, but without a commercial return and ended by auctioning the whole operation two years later. The purchasers, Turton Moor Coal Co seemed beset by accidents and by changes of directors before finally ceasing production in 1876, although they did succeed in exploiting fireclay as well as coal and in increasing the size of the operation to the extent that employed 36 men and boys in 1871. At least they were able to select the better parts of the seam and to maintain continuous production for 12 years.

Finally in 1892 came an attempt to increase the scale of operations by employing more men and investing in a new works. It was a bold move and soon led to large debts becoming too much for some of the shareholders. The resulting reorganisation, in 1900, allowed many of them to depart and left Darwen Sanitary Pipes Ltd. to carry on, and run into even more difficulties. By 1906 the mine seems to have been exhausted, little else was worth working on the 400 acre lease and in 1911 the company was wound up. Exactly how it managed between 1906 and 1911 is still not altogether clear, but it seems to have been with a much reduced output and without the use of Turton Moor Colliery.

Obviously the coal and fireclay reserves were too small to support the last stage of operations. They were probably barely enough to support the earlier operation that ended in 1876. Perhaps Andrew Knowles had the right idea. By 1855 he must have realised the limitations of the deposit, even for his modest operation. His company, after all, had much better and more extensive coal seams to work elsewhere and was on its way to becoming the biggest and perhaps best mining company in the country, but then Andrew Knowles had a reputation for making shrewd judgements.

All these events are now long past and there is little chance of mining being resumed in the area, for which most people are probably thankful. However it is perhaps worth trying to imagine what might have happened had the Lower Mountain Mine been rather more widespread and a little thicker. Then the pipe making would have lasted longer, been on a bigger scale and offered even more employment. Convenient accommodation for rent might well have been made available for the workforce, perhaps in the form of some 100 or more houses erected along the main road beyond Dimple, no doubt in stone terraces, together with a few shops, a public house and perhaps a chapel; a rail siding might even have been extended from near Chapeltown up to the pipe works. With enough growth development between Dimple and Darwen could have become almost continuous and the map of this part of Lancashire might have been quite different.

 But all this is mere conjecture, reality has been very different and despite all the coal and fireclay extracted from Turton Moor over the years, the long term effect has been so small that few people realise these activities ever occurred.

Montcliffe Colliery, Horwich: one of the last local fireclay producers.
(Upper) No 1 shaft with original wooden headframe c. 1960.
(Lower) No2 shaft in 1966, with steel headframe and stockpiles of fireclay left to 'weather'. The colliery closed soon after this photograph was taken.

REFERENCES

Government Mining Records
List of Mines, Geological Survey of Great Britain: published annually 1854-1880.
Report of the Inspector of Mines, List of Mines, published annually 1881- 1909.
Abandonment Plan: Coal Authority Plan No 86, Turton Moor Colliery 1878.

Board of Trade Company Records
Turton Moor Sanitary Pipe Co. 1893: Public Record Office, BT31/5648.
Darwen Sanitary Pipe Co. 1901: Public Record Office, BT31/9371.

Rating and Estate Valuations
Valuation of Turton Manor, 1831: LRO, UDTu19.
Turton Valuation, 1837: Bolton Archive, PTU.
Turton Rating Valuation, 1849: Bolton Archive, PTU11/2. 1866: LRO, UDTu18/28.

Local Authority
Letter from Briggs and Walsh, 1863: Bolton Archive, UDPTu11/2.
Letters in Turton Local Board and UDC Letter Book 1893-1904: LRO, UDTu3/5-7
  pp 39,42,194, 236 ,292.
Turton UDC Minutes: LRO, Feb 1903, UDTu6/1: April 1905, UDTu6/4: May 1906, UDTu6/5.

Directories
Bolton Directories !870/1, 1874.
Bolton Post Office Directories, 1894-1904.
Barret's Blackburn Directory, 1906.

Notices of Auctions
Bolton Chronicle: 7 Aug. 1852, p 4, col 4.
Bolton Chronicle: 21 Jan 1871, p 4, col 3.
Darwen News: 16,20,23 Feb 1901.

Press Articles
Bolton Chronicle: 23 April 1853, p 5, col 2.
Bolton Chronicle: 11 March 1865, p 8, col 5.
Bolton Chronicle: 19 October 1867. p 8, col 6.
Bolton Journal: 26 June 1875.
Darwen News: 16 February 1908 P 8.
Darwen News: 16 & 23 March 1901.
Colliery Guardian: 14 Sept 1861 p164-165.

Other Publications
Industrial Heritage of Darwen: M Rothwell, Bridgestone Press 1992.
Coal Mining in Salford: Geoff Preece, City of Salford Cultural Services 1985.

Maps
OS Lancashire 6in. (1:10560): Sheet 78 1849 Edition.
OS Lancashire 6in. (1:10560): Sheets 78NE and 78SE 1910 Edition.
OS Lancashire 25in. (1:2250) Sheets 78.12 and 78.8 1891 Edition.
OS Lancashire 25in. (1:2250) Sheets 78.12 and 78.8 1911 Edition.
Geol Survey Lancashire 6in. (1:10560) Sheet 78 1869 Edition.
Geol Survey Lancashire 6in. (1:10560) Sheets 78NE and 78SE 1936 Edition.